Original title:
Sharks of the Deep

Copyright © 2025 Creative Arts Management OÜ
All rights reserved.

Author: James
ISBN HARD
ISBN

Depths of Lurking Legends

In the blue, they glide with glee,
With toothy grins, oh so carefree.
They swirl in circles, dance about,
Chasing tails, what is that about?

Their fins like sails upon the tide,
With silly moves, they take great pride.
They peek through reefs, but oh so shy,
Playing hide and seek, 'cause that's their vibe!

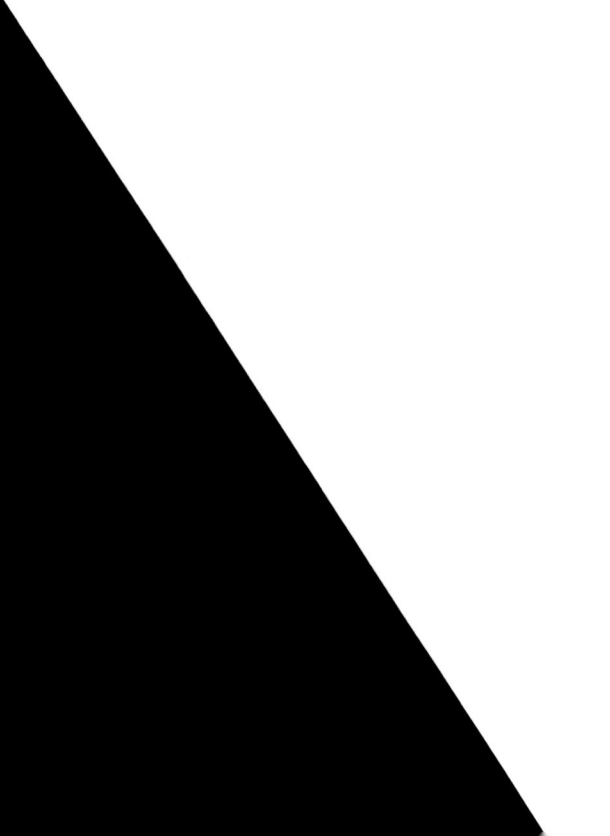

Water's Fearsome Guardians

Beneath the waves, the big ones swoop,
In goofy ways, they form a troop.
With bulging eyes and flappy flair,
They zoom and zoom, without a care.

Oh, what a sight, a finned parade,
In bubbled laughter, they're not afraid.
They strike a pose, hold still for fun,
Then dash away, just on the run!

The Specter of the Pelagic Night

In moonlit waters, shadows play,
The jokesters of the ocean sway.
With silly grins, they dart and twist,
A laughter echo in the mist.

They sneak up close, then whirl around,
In silly circles, they are found.
They wave their fins, a friendly tease,
Like underwater clowns, they do as they please!

Beneath Turbulent Waves

When storms arise and bubbles burst,
The wacky ones are known to thirst.
For all the ruckus and the fun,
A splashy race, they're on the run!

Skimming through kelp, they laugh and play,
Chasing each other in a silly way.
With faces wide and tales to spin,
They're the jesters, with toothy grins!

Mystic Predators of the Midnight Sea

In shadows lurk with toothy grins,
They dance and splash like silly twins.
With fins that slice, they glide and dive,
Creating chaos, oh how they thrive!

Beneath the waves, they hold a show,
Wearing crowns made of seaweed, oh so low.
They chuckle as they swim with might,
Who knew they could be such a sight?

Swirling round like whirlwinds' glee,
Playing tag with fish, oh what a spree!
With gaping jaws, they grin and wink,
Ocean jesters in water's drink.

So if you hear a giggle or screech,
It's not just fish, but their wild speech.
In nighttime hues, the mischief grows,
These silly beasts not everyone knows!

Secrets from Ocean's Cradle

In deep blue beds where secrets lie,
The creatures scheme, oh my, oh my!
With bubble hats and pouting lips,
They plot their mischief from their ships.

They frolic round in sandy groves,
Telling tales of their underwater troves.
With laughter bubbling like the sea,
These playful ghouls swim wild and free.

Count the teeth, but not so fast,
They're sharper than a sailor's cast.
But with a wink and silly dance,
They'll lure you in with a comic prance.

From shadows thick to sunlit beams,
They dream of fish and silly schemes.
With every splash, a riddle born,
In ocean's cradle, laughter's sworn!

Kindred of the Dark Waters

In suits of gray and toothy grins,
They glide like dancers, where the fun begins.
With tails that swish and bubble gum,
They tease the fish—oh, what have they done?

With every twist, they share a laugh,
Beneath the waves, they have the final guffaw.
A finny troupe of clumsy cheer,
Sipping on seaweed–that's the real beer!

An Ocean's Dance of Fear

They waltz around in playful fright,
With silly grins, oh what a sight!
Chasing bubbles like they're lost balloons,
Who knew the sea had such funny tunes?

With every snap and playful chase,
They weave through reefs with the utmost grace.
Clumsily pirouetting through the blue,
These jester fish have jokes, it's true!

The Echoing Silence of the Abyss

In the silent depths where shadows creep,
Those silly giants never sleep.
They play hide and seek with scared little rays,
And crack up laughing in mysterious ways.

With goofy poses and silly ties,
They pop their head up to the surface skies.
Like underwater clowns in a sea of gloom,
They're having a party in their watery room!

Veins of the Blue Wild

Through blue veins and swirling tides,
The jesters swim where humor abides.
With mischief brewing in every glance,
They start a ruckus—a bubbly dance!

They flap their fins, a comical sight,
As bubbles burst, they giggle with delight.
The ocean floor shakes with laughter so deep,
The wild ones plunge into a giggling heap!

Goliaths of the Coastal Abyss

Beneath the waves, they twirl and play,
Big teeth flashing in a goofy display.
In water parks, they'd win the race,
With a splash, they'd steal the show, what a face!

Munching on fish like it's their lunch,
They giggle in gills, blissfully in a bunch.
A circus act beneath the tide,
Every flip and twist, they take with pride.

Secrets of the Deep Currents

In the dark where bubbles dance and swirl,
They hide the secrets in a giggly whirl.
With a wink and a nod, they plot their schemes,
Making fishy faces, living in dreams.

They swipe the seashells, laugh out loud,
In their underwater kingdom, they feel so proud.
A tickle of fins, it's a comedic plot,
Making even grumpy crabs lose their snot!

Elegy of the Finned Hunters

Oh the finned ones, with their silly grins,
In the deep, they chase their watery fins.
With a flappy dance, they swirl in delight,
Leaving bubbles of laughter, a joyful sight.

Too cool for school, they strut on the reef,
Chasing their tails, they forget their grief.
Each pursuit a game, the ocean their stage,
In this finned comedy, they write their page.

The Abyssal Serenade

A serenade rises where the sun don't peek,
With tunes of giggles from the salty cheek.
They serenade schools, in the deep they sway,
Making fish giggle as they float and play.

In the velvet depths, with a splash and a swirl,
The sea's finest jesters invite you to twirl.
Join the party, don't miss the beat,
For the jesters of the sea bring laughs so sweet!

Silent Predators

In the ocean, they glide with glee,
Fins that dance and twist like a spree.
With teeth that sparkle, oh so bright,
They grin at fish, who take to flight.

With a swish of tails, they show off more,
Imitating dolphins, but what's in store?
Jaws that open like a big old door,
But they prefer sushi, oh what a chore!

They sneak up close, with a playful grace,
Making waves, but never a race.
Whispers in water, it's a jolly song,
Just hoping, the fish guess right or wrong.

So, cheers to the kings of the brine and blue,
Who think they're scary, but really just chew.
In their misunderstood, finned escapade,
They're the comedians in the underwater parade.

Underwater Shadows

In the deep where the shadows play,
Gliding in style, they steal the day.
With a flick of their fins, they take a chance,
Trying to lead a fishy dance.

They sneak up close, looking for some fun,
A tickle or two, then they run!
Their grins so wide, they crack a jest,
Making the ocean a funny fest.

Darts and twists, a suave ballet,
Chasing bubbles, bubbles that sway.
"Catch me if you can!" they seem to shout,
But it's the fish that are left in doubt.

In the murky depths, laughter whirls,
As fins become the laughter curls.
They might be fierce, or so we're told,
But their goofy antics are pure gold.

Echoes of the Abyss

From the depths comes a humorous boom,
A giggle gurgle, echoing the gloom.
With mouths agape, they swim around,
Prepping punchlines, silly sounds.

Stealthy gliders, with grins so sly,
They whisper jokes, then pass them by.
Who knew a gaping maw held such cheer?
An underwater comedy show right here!

Echoes of laughter, in the blue so deep,
Not a single fish will ever sleep.
With quips and quirks, they entertain,
While the clownfish roll, free from the strain.

In a watery world where giggles reside,
It's the jokesters who take us for a ride.
Just a pinch of humor, the ocean's gift,
In the abyss, they give our spirits a lift.

Gliding Titans

Gliding through waves, oh what a sight,
With swagger and smiles, they own the night.
Titanic creatures, but not so tough,
In their giant presence, they're just a bit buff.

Jaws wide open, but not for a munch,
More for a laugh or a goofy punch.
Riding the currents, they joke and jive,
In the grand sea circus, they twist and dive.

With a swish of a tail, they spread the cheer,
Laughing at fish that swim in fear.
A playful nudge, a gentle tease,
In this watery world, they aim to please.

So let's celebrate the comedy queens,
Of the deep blue—a party of scenes.
Titanic and funny, with a wink and a grin,
In their bubbling laughter, where joy begins.

Echoes from the Big Blue

In the ocean's vast embrace,
Fish wear puzzled looks,
For beneath the gentle waves,
A toothy grin hooks!

Bubbles burst in glee,
In a dance so silly,
With fins that flutter fast,
Making all feel frilly!

Trust not the dark of night,
When laughter hides within,
For a fellow with a wink,
Shows off his toothy grin!

In troubles deep and wide,
With goofy tales to share,
The tales of finned jesters,
Who swim without a care!

The Silent Chase

Underneath the wavy tide,
A mystery, oh so sly,
With bubbles popping loud,
A fish does a backflip high!

Chasing after friend or foe,
With a zigzag here and there,
In a game of hide and seek,
Fins flapping everywhere!

Giggling in the sunlit sea,
As frothy waves dance near,
A playful splish and splash,
Bringing laughter, joy and cheer!

But watch your tasty snacks,
For they'll disappear in haste,
When a sneaky grin appears,
Hiding hunger with a taste!

Fabled Beasts of the Void

Legends swirl in ocean tales,
Of creatures wise and spry,
With goofy looks on fishy faces,
As they swim and fly!

They're not here for a feast,
But to tickle and tease,
With winks and gags, and silly jigs,
Oh, they'll never cease!

In the shadows they do schmooze,
With tricks and playful spins,
Their laughter echoes loud and clear,
As the underwater fun begins!

So come and join the jolly tide,
Where laughter runs so deep,
With fabled friends who'll keep you guessing,
In secrets they will keep!

The Enigmatic Blue

In waters vast and curious,
Life swirls in strange delight,
With creatures dressed in comedy,
Entering the playful night!

With flicks and flutters, jests unfold,
In aquatic masquerade,
Where every fin is up to tricks,
And chuckles will invade!

Dive into the depths unknown,
With mirth beneath the waves,
For unknown beasts and silly pranks,
Are what the ocean braves!

So come along, let's take a plunge,
Into this goofy spree,
With friends of fins and laughter roars,
In the enigmatic sea!

Specters of the Sea Breeze

In the ocean's grand parade,
A fin spins round, a silly charade.
With a toothy grin that's wide,
They glide through waves on a joyous ride.

With bubble-blowing ease, they tease,
Chasing fish with playful pleas.
Their laughter echoes, gurgling songs,
Making splashy waves where each one belongs.

An old sea turtle joins the fun,
As plankton twirls, the party's begun.
With flip-flops on their fins, what a game!
These sea jesters are far from tame.

So if you dip your toes just right,
You may see them pirouette in delight.
With jiggly dances, they enchant the sea,
Specters of joy, come play with me!

Abyssal Requiem

In the dark, where few will tread,
A jester swims with disco dread.
With sparkles in their watchful eye,
They hold a court, where giggles fly.

Their friends are quirky, costumes bright,
They boogie down in the deep night.
A conga line of critters' glee,
With seaweed hats, who could disagree?

A flash of teeth, a goofy grin,
In the silence, the laughter begins.
They munch on kelp, like pop corn treats,
In the realm where the sea monster meets.

So remember, next time you swim,
There's a party where lights grow dim.
With every fin, the fun ignites,
A requiem of joy in oceanic nights.

The Power Beneath

In the depths, where shadows play,
A funky crew makes waves today.
With wiggly tails and wacky styles,
They dance around in goofy piles.

The currents pull, the bubbles pop,
As you giggle at the flip-flop shop.
An octopus paints a wild mural,
While pals join in for the great swirl.

Each fin a brush, each splash a smile,
Making art that spans a mile.
With belly laughs and silly snorts,
In this deep, the joy consorts.

So don't you fret when you dive down,
For beneath the waves, there's no frown.
A party lurks just out of sight,
With ocean's power and sheer delight.

Fins Beneath the Waves

Underneath the rolling tides,
A merry band of fins abides.
With turtlenecks and jelly shoes,
They recreate the latest blues.

They twirl and spin, each curve a flare,
A splatter of joy in the salty air.
With seafood snacks, their feast is grand,
As krills and shrimps make up the band.

With silly chases and tickled toes,
They leap through spaces, where laughter flows.
Each puff of bubbles is a cue,
To dance around, join in the crew.

So when you float on a sunny day,
Just listen close, and you might sway.
For in the depths, where fun survives,
The zany spirit of joy thrives.

Nightfall in the Coral Castles

In castles bright where fish do dwell,
A playful giant bids farewell.
He wiggles through the coral maze,
With toothy grin that wildly plays.

The tiny clownfish scatter fast,
As laughter echoes from the past.
His fin a flag, a joyful sight,
In twilight's glow, a silly fright.

The seaweed sways, a dance they make,
From prank to prank, they twist and shake.
With bubble bursts and flicks of tail,
They turn the ocean into a trail.

So dive beneath the moon's soft gleam,
Where laughter runs like a bubbling stream.
In coral halls of pure delight,
A funny dance ignites the night.

Water's Silent Assassins

In depths where giants glide about,
They play hide and seek, without a doubt.
With fins like ninjas, stealthy, sly,
They sneak around, oh me, oh my!

With a backflip here, a wiggle there,
They splash and swish, so unaware.
The crabs do giggle, oh what a show,
As masked with bubbles, they're all aglow.

Mischief follows like a shadowed dance,
While fish in silver twirl and prance.
They chase their tails in a gleeful race,
In watery realms, they find their place.

So next time you're by the ocean's sway,
Look closely; they're just a splash away.
In realms of blue, they jest and play,
Water's jesters brighten the day.

A Dance in the Pelagic Realm

In oceans wide, where laughter blooms,
A party starts in shaded tombs.
With swirls and twirls, they take the floor,
A pelagic dance, an endless chore.

Their partners glide, a wiggly charm,
They spin and dart, there's no alarm.
With a twist of fin and cheeky flaunt,
They swirl like leaves in an ocean jaunt.

The jellies bounce with jelly giggles,
While fishes snag with silly wriggles.
In currents gentle, they flap like sails,
All join the tune of aquatic tales.

So join the swirl, don't be too shy,
In this great sea, where spirits fly.
Just take a dip, let worries cease,
A dance awaits, a splash of peace.

Tides of the Ancient Predators

Old legends tell of finned delights,
With bloated bellies, they're out at night.
With toothy smiles and goofy grins,
They're kings of pranks, as laughter spins.

With ancient eyes, they plot and scheme,
As unsuspecting fish chase a dream.
But wait—oh no! It's just a show,
Their sneaky ways make giggles flow.

A silly chase through coral glades,
With flaps and flops, they steal parades.
The ocean roars with laughter bright,
In tides that twirl under starlit night.

So swim along with joy in store,
Join in the fun; there's always more.
In depths where ancient spirits roam,
You'll find the sea is their true home.

Guardians of the Dark Blue

In suits of gray, they glide with flair,
With toothy grins, they take the dare.
They dance with fish in ocean's ball,
Not caring if they sometimes fall.

With tiny fins, they play their game,
Pretending that they're quite the same.
In seaweed capes, they twirl about,
Rolling with laughter, not a doubt.

They boast of size, a grand display,
Yet hide behind the coral fray.
A wink, a spin, they go for gold,
In tales of glory, never old.

So when you dive and take a peek,
Don't fear the big, don't feel the weak.
For in this blue, a joke's the key,
They're just performers, wild and free.

Titans of the Submerged Realm

In waters deep where shadows loom,
They reign supreme, their jaws a bloom.
With silly grins, they strike a pose,
The ocean's kings in finny clothes.

They swim in circles, plot and plan,
To steal a snack from any man.
But when they're full, they do a dance,
A wiggly, giggly ocean prance.

With every turn, a splash and flick,
They joke around, they're quite the trick.
Pretending fear, they wear a mask,
But love to play, that's all they ask.

Through currents swift, they laugh and tease,
Chasing bubbles, dancing with ease.
The titans of the ocean blue,
Just having fun, as titans do.

Monstrous Migrations

In schools they roam, a wiggly lot,
With tales of grandeur, they're quite the shot.
From here to there, they make a fuss,
A traveling circus, riding the bus.

They flap their fins, a sight to see,
In search of snacks, perhaps some brie.
An endless quest to find a treat,
Beware the conga line, oh what a feat!

Their destinations? Where the fish are ripe,
But sometimes end in a comedy type.
Bumbling and tumbling, they break in glee,
Misdirection's their key to spree.

So gear up for the show of the year,
As they parade with splashes and cheer.
Monstrous, yes, but with hearts so light,
Adventurous spirits, ready to bite.

Depths' Predatory Grace

In the murky depths where laughter grows,
They glide with grace, in swirling flows.
A grin so wide, as bright as day,
Turning all fears into playful sway.

They may look fierce with those shining teeth,
But underneath lurks a jokester's wreath.
With every chase, a playful jest,
Life's just a game, they're truly blessed.

With striking moves, they twirl and whirl,
Showing off swirls like a dolphin's twirl.
In moments of thrill, they share a laugh,
Creating a fun and epic craft.

So if you dive into their domain,
Just know that joy is never mundane.
For with every fin that flaps and sways,
They're teaching us all how fun it plays.

Creatures of the Midnight Waters

In the depths where shadows play,
Fin-tastic folks come out to sway.
With toothy grins and silly dances,
They twirl around with playful prances.

Bubbles burst with laughter loud,
As they gather for a fishy crowd.
Wit and whirls in the ocean's hall,
Who knew they had such a ball?

What's that swooshing, what's that sound?
It's a wiggly party going round!
With every splash and silly flip,
They make the big blue feel like a trip!

So if you hear a giggle glee,
Know there's fun beneath the sea.
These merry mischief-makers thrive,
In the midnight waters, they come alive!

Legends of the Abyss

Down where legends creep and crawl,
The finned ones echo a goofy call.
Tales of treasure and rivalries,
Yet all they want is some good cheese!

Once a giant lost his way,
He tried to sit on a coral bay.
But with a pop and a squatter's cheer,
He sent a wave and made snacks appear!

Dreams of battles, they try to spin,
But really, they're just grinning within.
Who needs glory or golden crowns?
When the ocean's fun can flip your frowns!

So raise a fin to the tales so tall,
Of the jolly ones that rise and fall.
In the vastness of the gloomy blue,
Laughter reigns, and it's all for you!

The Sovereign Swimmers

Majestic glide of the merry fleet,
In snazzy suits, they think they're neat.
Sporty fins and smiles so wide,
In their kingdom, they take the ride.

With goofy grins, they claim the throne,
Making mischief when they're alone.
Racing bubbles 'long the way,
Chasing tails in a splashy display!

They strut their stuff with a royal flair,
Twisting, turning, without a care.
As kings and queens of the blue abyss,
They rule with joy, we can't dismiss!

So join the fun, dive joyously,
In the realm of these finned royalty.
With every wave and every cheer,
These sovereign swimmers have nothing to fear!

Veiled Beasts of the Ocean

Beneath the surface, quite the sight,
Veiled figures dance, oh what a fright!
But peek a bit closer, and what do you see?
Just playful pals sipping on sea tea!

They dodge and weave like clumsy ninjas,
In a swirling ballet, no time for cringes.
With tentacles waving, they play tag,
But trip on themselves like a comical rag!

Each sneaky flip, each gurgly sound,
Shows that fun's the best game around.
In curious masks, they jest and play,
Making each moment a vibrant display!

So if you catch a glimpse so rare,
Of these veiled jokers without a care,
Just know they laugh with ocean's grace,
In the depths, they create their own space!

Symphony of the Abyssal Hunters

In the ocean's dark, where creatures glide,
Bubbles puff out, fish try to hide.
With toothy grins and tails that swish,
They're on a hunt, oh, what a fish!

Fins flap about in a dance so grand,
Making waves like a seaside band.
They sing their tunes in a gurgling way,
Chasing their dinner, oh what a play!

With wiggly moves and a dash of flair,
They zoom on past without a care.
Each splash a giggle, a watery jest,
In this underwater comedy fest!

Munching on snacks in a curvy twirl,
They swirl around in a giggly whirl.
These hunters of night, with a laugh and a wink,
Make every dive a jolly blink!

Beneath the Moonlit Waves

Underneath the gleam of a silver light,
Mischief brews in the watery night.
Creatures frolic, with eyes all aglow,
Poking at crabs, putting on a show!

With wiggly tails doing flips and spins,
They tease the octopus, in for a grin.
The seaweed sways like a dance floor bright,
Swaying together in a playful fight.

Tickling the clams, just for good fun,
Playing tag till the morning sun.
A splash here, a splash there, oh what a scene,
Life's a party, if you know what I mean!

Beneath the waves, laughter does float,
A merry crew in a fishy boat.
With bubbles of joy, they glide and they zoom,
While the moon plays on, lighting up the room!

Predators in the Stillness

In silent depths where shadows creep,
A toothy grin stirs from its sleep.
With sneaky moves and winks so sly,
It's snack time now, oh my oh my!

They glide on by in a crafty way,
Chasing the fish like a game of tag play.
A twist, a turn, they spin and dash,
Beneath the waves, there's quite a splash!

With jellyfish flapping and crabs in fright,
They create a ruckus in the quiet night.
Each munch and crunch, a giggling cheer,
The rulers of laughter, never a fear!

While bubbles escape like laughter anew,
They frolic and glide in a whirlpool view.
In the stillness reigns a cheeky crew,
A comedy sketch in the ocean blue!

Tides of the Unseen

In the depths, there's a rumor, a funny scene,
With laughter echoing, if you know what I mean.
They sneak and they slide on a moonlit ride,
Playing hide and seek, with no reason to hide.

With wiggly tails and bubbly grins,
They chase each other, let the antics begin!
A splash here, a flip there, with fins all aglow,
A comedy of errors in the depths, oh so low!

The tides roll in with a giggle and cheer,
As the ocean's jesters swim far and near.
Each little scare is but part of the play,
In the vast watery world, come join the fray!

So beneath the waves, where laughter will bloom,
The tides of the unseen clear up all gloom.
With friends to frolic and jest by your side,
In the deep, oh, what fun—come take the ride!

Nature's Veiled Warriors

In suits of armor, they glide with grace,
The ocean's lawyers, without a face.
With toothy grins and playful bites,
They dance through bubbles, in swirling lights.

Sneaky sleek, with a glinting eye,
They munch on fish as they zoom by.
"Hey, that's my snack!" a fishy pleads,
But in this game, it's about who leads.

In a coral castle, they throw a ball,
Where seaweed curtains and sea snails crawl.
With feathery friends, they twirl and sway,
While posing for selfies at the break of day.

So if you see them, don't run away,
Just wave and cheer for their ocean play.
For nature's jesters, forever we greet,
In this comical realm of the salty treat.

Chasing Shadows in the Sea

Beneath the waves, they plot and scheme,
Fishy dreams in a tangled dream.
With a flick of a fin, they take a spin,
Who knew deep blues could be such a win?

Eels look on with a jealous frown,
As they glide through reefs, like a circus brown.
"Catch me if you can!" they challenge a ray,
In a slapstick race, with no time to play.

Ocean's jesters, swift on their feet,
Bubbles erupt in laughter, quite the feat!
With silly antics that charm and delight,
They paint joy in the dark, a whimsical sight.

So dive in deep, where the laughter flows,
In a bubbly world where mischief grows.
With smiles and giggles all around,
In the crescent moon's beam, happiness is found.

Rulers of the Inky Depths

In the black abyss with a royal air,
They reign with flair, quite beyond compare.
With regal tails and a cheeky grin,
They wear their crowns, let the antics begin!

Chasing crabs like they're fast new shoes,
Engaging in games, there's nothing to lose.
"Who's got the best flips?" they argue with glee,
In royal splendor, beneath the sea.

A banquet spread of treasures abound,
Where seashells chatter and giggles resound.
Oh what a feast, with snacks piled high,
In their underwater empire, no one's shy!

So keep your eyes peeled for the jesters in blue,
As they twirl and swirl in a bubbly queue.
For the rulers of depths don't take things too hard,
In a world of laughter, they'll keep up the guard!

The Sea's Untamed Sentinels

Guardians of laughter, with hearts full of cheer,
They splash through the waves, oh so dear.
With swirling twists and daring leaps,
In the grand theater where laughter keeps.

They sing silly songs about stinky feet,
While performing tricks that can't be beat.
"Join us!" they holler, "The fun's just begun,"
In a whimsical whirl where all can run.

With wiggly tails and a playful chase,
They tag their friends in a bubbly race.
Under the sun, they play hide and seek,
In an ocean playground, loud and unique.

So let's celebrate these carefree souls,
In their watery realm, where joy extols.
With laughter and fun, they elude the mundane,
In a merry ballet under the ocean's reign.

Shadows of the Trench

In the watery depths, where the mischief swims,
Jaws wide as a door, but they're just like whims.
With a grin on their face and a twinkle in eye,
They'll steal your sandwich, oh my, oh my!

Fins flap and they wiggle, such sleek little spies,
Chasing after bubbles, while plotting surprise.
"Is that a fish platter?" one giggles with glee,
Grabbing hot fries while they jiggle and flee!

They rush through the darkness, playing truth or dare,
"Who can do ballet in these waters so rare?"
A whirl of pinches and playful taunts,
They leave you all laughing—oh, what funny haunts!

So if you should wander where the shadows loom,
Beware of the jesters with fins that consume.
They'll tickle your toes and might nibble your snack,
But deep in their hearts, they just want a laugh back!

Twilight Hunters Below

At dusk, when the sea turns to shimmering night,
Comes a band of pranksters ready for a fight.
With eyes full of mischief and gills set to tease,
They float through the water with such graceful ease.

"Hey, is that a shark?" one whispers with cheer,
"Or just a big fish with a mustache and beard?"
They giggle and tumble, their shadows so sly,
With giggles and splashes, oh how they fly!

Their dreams made of bubble gum and cake,
Chasing each other, watching their wake.
"Whose turn is it next to wear that cool hat?"
A game of the silliest—splash, thump, and splat!

So next time you're swimming, just keep a close watch,
For the clowns of the twilight with smiles that you'll botch.
They're not here for trouble, just laughter and fun,
Dancing through currents 'til the day is done!

Mirage of the Deep Waters

In the deep blue where the bubbles play,
Lives a crew of jesters who dance through the spray.
With hats made of seaweed and tails that can twirl,
They spin and they swirl, oh what a world!

"Who can do flips?" one says with a grin,
"What's better than swimming? Let's dive right in!"
They leap through the waves with laughter and cheer,
Making sure no one feels a hint of fear.

With pizzazz and style, they glide with great flair,
Chasing their shadows, catching sea air.
Their stories are silly, their antics absurd,
With trickster hearts, they fly like a bird.

So if you should plunge into waters quite deep,
And see merry creatures in a giddy heap,
Just know they're the jesters of tides elemental,
Bringing joy to the ocean, it's all accidental!

Ocean's Silent Phantoms

In twilight's embrace, where the waters do flow,
Lurk the giggling phantoms, all covered in glow.
With shimmery smiles and a wiggle so grand,
They play hide and seek through the sea's shimmering sand.

"Look at me wiggle!" one whispers so low,
"I just tripped on a rock—oh, how did that go?"
They tumble and roll in the surf's frothy laugh,
Creating a ruckus, a slippery gaffe!

Like shadows that dance in the hush of the tide,
They whisper of secrets that time cannot hide.
If you ever should wander where the bubbles erupt,
Watch out for these phantoms who merrily disrupt!

For under the moonlight, their pranks have no peep,
They'll tickle your toes while you drift off to sleep.
In the ocean's embrace, their giggles will bloom,
Hiding in silence, they'll plot your next zoom!

Emissaries of the Black Depths

In the dark, they do waddle,
With a grin that's quite a coddle.
Sneaking snacks from sailors' nets,
These clumsy swimmers are the best bets.

With a fin that's just a bit too large,
They're on a mission to take charge.
Dancing shadows in the gloom,
Where every shark thinks it can zoom.

A toothy grin, a bubble bath,
Catching krill, they're on the path.
They giggle while they glide and sway,
Playing hide and seek all day.

Riding waves, they set the pace,
In their underwater race.
No worries of a fishy snack,
Just here for laughs, they'll never lack.

Silent Shadows Beneath

In the depths where silence reigns,
Float the legends with funny claims.
Whispers of teeth when they swim by,
"Did you see me, oh my my!"

Gliding past in dreamy hues,
They sip on algae, sharing news.
"Did you hear the one 'bout the whale?"
They roll with laughter, start to flail.

With eyes as wide as their big dreams,
They're the rulers of silly schemes.
A splash here, a twirl and spin,
In this world, the smiles begin.

Tales of snags and close mishaps,
"And then I nearly lost my cap!"
Beneath the waves, they're laughing loud,
In the ocean's depths, they're so proud.

Cunning Chasers of the Sea

The ocean's jesters, sleek and sly,
Catch the currents, oh how they fly!
With a twirl and a wink, they take a dive,
In games of tag, they sure thrive.

They peek from rocks and wiggle their tails,
Telling stories of shipwrecked sails.
"Boo!" they shout, with a playful cheer,
In the sea's grand circus, they are near.

Poking their noses in each nook,
Like mischievous kids with a brand new book.
Each splash a giggle, every turn a tease,
Chasing bubbles with absolute ease.

The cunning ones with laughter bright,
Hiding in shadows till it's bite.
But fear not, for they just want to play,
In their silly, fishy ballet.

Teeth of the Tide

With pearly whites and a cheeky grin,
These fibrous friends roll out to win.
Popcorn shrimp and silly snacks,
They munch away, no thought of fracks.

They jingle and jangle as they roam,
In the big blue sea, they call it home.
"Did you see that crab? It's such a joke!"
Laughter echoes, like a yoke.

Under the waves, they've got their style,
Snapping jaws that flash and smile.
Tide's teeth chatter, what a blast,
Dancing playfully, swimming fast.

So if you hear a splash and clatter,
It's just these friends, a little chatter.
In the ocean's realm, they're quite the sight,
Teeth of the tide, oh what a delight!

The Talons Beneath

With fins like knives and grins so wide,
They glide beneath with laughter, sly.
Jaws that snap and tickle too,
I think they're ready for a game of boo!

In the moonlight, they dance and play,
What a sight, their finned ballet!
Chasing fish in a swirling spree,
Is it a fish fry or a party for three?

Their shadows loom, a wiggly tease,
With playful nudges in the breeze.
They'll steal your lunch with a cheeky grin,
And leave you giggling, where to begin?

So plunge with glee, don't be afraid,
They're masters of fun in their underwater parade.
Just keep your snacks close to your chest,
For those talons beneath love a tasty fest!

Guardians of the Twilight Waters

In the twilight pool where creatures quake,
They guard the tides with a giddy shake.
Bubbles burst and ripples gleam,
Oh look, it's a fishy dream team!

Fins waving wildly like flags in flight,
They throw a party to delight the night.
With cheeky flips and twists so neat,
Those guardians groove to the ocean's beat.

A tickle with a tail, oh what a sight,
They bring the jazz to the deep, deep night.
With a wink and a grin, they glide right by,
As the moon shines down, and fish swim shy.

So if you swim and hear a cackle,
Join the fun, don't you dawdle!
The twilight waters are theirs to keep,
Where laughter echoes and secrets sleep.

The Ocean's Eternal Watchers

They survey the waves with perky flair,
With eyes like saucers, they're always aware.
Making faces, they swim with class,
What a splash when you see them pass!

With whistles and giggles, they greet the tide,
In a friendly wave, they take great pride.
Curly cues and twirls aplenty,
Their silly antics drive all fish giddy.

Oh, wise guardians of the depths so wide,
They'll tell you tales with a glimmering glide.
From fishy pranks to treasure chests,
No ocean lingers without their jests!

So dive in close, don't miss the chance,
To join their playful underwater dance.
With a wink and a splash, they make it clear,
Fun's the treasure you'll find down here!

Symphony of the Deep

In the brush of the ocean, a tune takes flight,
With giggles and swirls, it feels just right.
They strut and they hum, a jazzy decree,
Underwater walls of cheeky glee!

With tails that tickle and bubbles that pop,
These merry musicians will never stop.
Each wave a note, each splash a beat,
In their symphony, life feels so sweet.

Starlit rhythms dance through the sea,
With every glide, they sing carefree.
Catch the breeze, feel the rhythm swell,
For in this deep, fun stories dwell.

So gather around, let the good vibes seep,
You're invited to join this jolly leap.
In the Symphony of the deep, you'll see,
The ocean's laughter, wild and free!

Creatures of Night's Embrace

In the black, they swim and glide,
Jaws a'grin, they take it in stride.
With silly dances, they can't compete,
Swaying like they've got two left feet.

Ticklish fins and goofy scales,
Rolling past with frothy snails.
They can't help but grin and wave,
Pretending they're all so brave.

Their shadows loom, but don't you fret,
They've got jokes you won't forget.
With bubbles that make silly sounds,
These jesters of the sea abound.

So if you spot a toothy grin,
Know it's just a laugh within.
For in the night they play and tease,
Cackling 'neath the starlit breeze.

Lords of the Ocean's Abyss

In the deep where light stays shy,
Silly kings just float on by.
With crowns of kelp atop their heads,
They rule with giggles, not with dread.

Fins that flutter, tails that sway,
They mime a dance in a comical way.
Bubbles bursting in a flurry,
Quick to joke, never in a hurry.

With toothy grins and wide-eyed glee,
They tell tales of the great blue sea.
In their court, the laughter roars,
They banter 'til the ocean snores.

So fear not the lords down there,
They prance and play without a care.
For in their realm of dreams and fun,
They'll make you laugh 'til the night is done.

Whispers of the Ocean's Depths

In the quiet depths, where secrets sleep,
A chuckle dances, oh so deep.
With cheeky winks and playful swirls,
They swirl around like giddy girls.

Listen close, they'll crack a pun,
In bubble language, just for fun.
Silly whispers ride the waves,
While teasing tales the ocean saves.

With every wave, a giggle flows,
Even in shadows, laughter grows.
They spin and twirl, no sense of fear,
Making mischief, far and near.

So dive on down, join in their spree,
For in the depths, it's all about glee.
In whispers low, they'll share their dreams,
Of jelly dances and fishy schemes.

Sinister Gliders of the Sea

With a flick of a fin, they glide with grace,
But watch them closely, they'll put on a face.
Rolling their eyes in splendid delight,
With playful antics that bring pure fright.

Their beady eyes burst with delight,
As they spin and swirl, creating a fright.
But if you laugh, they'll beam with pride,
Chasing you down for a joyful ride.

They swoop and dive, making a scene,
Pretending to be the ocean's queen.
With carcass jokes and silliness rife,
They turn a horror into pure life.

So if you see them, don't scream or shout,
Join in the fun, that's what it's about!
With toothy grins and a sly little wink,
These gliders of sea make you rethink.

Legends of the Forgotten Sea

Once upon a time in the ocean blue,
Swam a curious creature with a toothy view.
He wore a top hat and danced with glee,
Making waves with his friends, oh what a spree!

They twirled and they twirled, avoiding the net,
In a game of tag, they'd never forget.
With seaweed confetti, they partied all night,
And giggled at bubbles that made quite a sight!

Some fish in tuxedos joined in the fun,
As jellyfish floated, shining like sun.
With a wink and a chuckle, they made quite a show,
In the ripping sea dance, where all madness would flow!

So if you dive deep where the legends do play,
You might find a creature who jests all day.
He'll tip his hat gently and swim right on by,
Winking and splashing as he waves you goodbye!

Shadows of the Forgotten Abyss

In the shadowy corners where mysteries lie,
Lurk fish in a hurry, oh my, oh my!
With goofy grins and oversized jaws,
They swim through the darkness with no pause!

One wore a monocle, it looked so chic,
While another tried to dance, but tripped on a reef.
They whispered of treasures that shimmered like gold,
But mostly just shared all their tales, bold and old.

"Did you hear about Larry?" one fish squeaked low,
"He found a lost shoe, but it stank like toe!"
They cackled and chortled, their laughter rang clear,
As the stories of folly brought them all cheer!

So, if you float down in the murky deep ends,
Remember the laughter of aquatic friends.
In shadows where giggles and silliness swirl,
There's a party aboard for each fin and whirl!

In the Grip of the Depths

In the chilly deep where the laughter is loud,
A fish in a bowtie swam straight through the crowd.
He juggled some clams while chewing on kelp,
Making everyone chuckle, what a strange help!

A crab with a top hat joined in the fun,
Gabbing and clapping till the day was done.
Beneath the dark waves, they danced with such flair,
Kicking up bubbles, oh, what a rare pair!

"Oh look, it's a mermaid with shoes made of pearls!"
They shouted and laughed, like mischievous swirls.
With a twinkling grin, she wiggled away,
Leaving them guessing, what a silly display!

So, down in the depths, where the humor flows free,
The underwater antics are all meant to be.
With joy in the currents, let's swim and explore,
For laughter is treasure, forever in store!

Whispers of the Abyssal Depths

In the depths so dark where the giggles abound,
There's an octopus named Fred, making mischief all round.
With eight wiggling arms, he painted the floor,
With polka-dot patterns, oh what a chore!

His pals all gathered, oh what a sight,
To see Fred's creations come to life in the night.
They chuckled and snickered, oh how they all played,
With fluorescent colors that Fred had displayed!

Through the gloom, they dashed with a glimmering glee,
Turning squishy creatures into art, oh whee!
They tickled the squids till they squirted the ink,
In the ocean's own canvas, they painted their stink!

So if you dive deep where the colors collide,
And listen for whispers that dance in the tide,
Know that in darkness, there's fun to be found,
In the laughter of critters, joy knows no bound!

Abyssal Dancers

In the dark where the giggles thrive,
Fins twirl and twist, oh how they jive.
With their toothy grins, they glide through green,
Dancing in shadows, like you've never seen.

Tentacles wiggle, a party down low,
Electric moves steal the deep sea show.
With a splash and a bloat, they take their stance,
Join the abyss with a frantic prance.

A fishy conga, a wiggly spin,
Plenty of pals, let the fun begin!
They laugh and they dart, no need for a cue,
In the depths they rumble, with a hullabaloo.

Bubble-blowing buddies, so silly and spry,
Doing the cha-cha beneath the blue sky.
In a seaweed tux, the rhythms they keep,
What a sight down below, oh what a leap!

Secrets of the Deep Sea

Under waves where the riddle lies,
Giggles and bubbles, oh what a surprise!
Mysterious beasts with a wink and a smirk,
Sneak through the reefs, when the humans lurk.

Peeking from kelp, with a curious glance,
Wiggly critters invite you to dance.
A treasure chest filled with chuckles, you'll see,
Mysteries swim, just swimming with glee.

Luminous critters with sparkle and flair,
Gliding and twisting, without a care.
They hold their secrets, so sly and so sly,
In the belly of the sea, where giggles fly high.

They whisper of laughter in currents they weave,
In the watery world, it's hard to believe.
So come hear the tales of the frolicsome knaves,
In this watery land where the humor behaves!

Chasing Currents

In the tides where the sillies roam,
Swimmers zipping, calling this home.
Bumping their noses, oh what a chase,
Fins flipping, flopping, in a wild race.

With bubbles and wiggles, they dash and dive,
Chasing the currents, feeling alive.
Fishy friends giggle, spinning around,
In this dance of waves, joy knows no bound.

Leaping like acrobats high in the sea,
Caught in the thrill, it's just jubilee.
A frosty reception, a splash and a leap,
Who knew the ocean could make you laugh deep?

So come for the ride, keep up with the beat,
In the currents of laughter, life can't be beat.
With each swirling eddy, the fun never ends,
Underwater camaraderie blooms with new friends!

Elegy for the Ocean's Giants

Oh mighty beasts who roam the deep,
With yawns so wide, they make us weep.
Their history written in bubbles and foam,
Legends of laughter, they call it their home.

With balletic grace, they drift and glide,
Telling old jokes with a wink, a ride.
Their shadows swirl, hiding from view,
In the theater of tides, where the laughter is true.

Let's not forget their silly old ways,
Cracking jokes in the ocean's haze.
Honoring laughter, their legacy beams,
As they swim through the waves, fulfilling our dreams.

So here's to the giants, with smiles so wide,
Dancing in currents, they never must hide.
In the sea of delight, their spirits shall thrive,
Always reminding us, humor's alive!

The Depths' Apex

In the ocean's great expanse,
Lives a critter that loves to prance.
With jagged teeth and silly dance,
Making fish flee at a single glance.

A toothy grin, a toothy stare,
Swimming round without a care.
Jellyfish giggle, crabs declare,
'Watch out, folks, we're in for a scare!'

Waves Whispering Fear

In the waves where shadows hide,
Creatures come with quite the ride.
They're more like puppies, full of pride,
Flipping fins, not one to chide.

With a swish and a swash, they zoom and glide,
Bubbles burst as they collide.
Fish giggle, trying to bide,
'Is it play or are we fried?'

Bane of the Coral Kingdom

In the reef, where colors bloom,
Dwells a beast that makes fish fume.
With a smile that could light a room,
It leaves the little ones in gloom.

Crown jewels swim, all in a hurry,
As this finned king causes such flurry.
With a roll, it brings such worry,
Fish proclaim, 'It's time to scurry!'

Slicing Through Darkness

In the depths where sunlight fades,
Lives a clown in finned cascades.
A master of all crushing trades,
Turning fish into lemonades!

With a flash and a mighty slice,
It twirls and dives, oh so nice.
The ocean giggles, adds some spice,
As critters flee, thinking twice!

Fins Beneath the Surface

In the ocean's vast embrace,
Fins wiggle with glee and grace.
With bubbles blowing in their wake,
They dance like goofy fishy flakes.

Swirling round with toothy grins,
These aquatic kings know how to spin.
A clumsy leap, a silly dive,
In their wavy world, all are alive.

They swirl together, a comic crew,
With antics that would make you woo-hoo!
Chasing seaweed, they don't care,
Who knew the ocean's got its flair?

So if you splash and take a dip,
Just know that they might join your trip.
Fins beneath with a joke or two,
Life's a laugh beneath the blue!

The Ocean's Hunters

Down where the bubbles pop and fizz,
There's a team of gliders, oh what a whizz!
With side-swept grins and playful yelps,
They're the ocean's goofiest kelp elves.

Sneaky sneaks with a toothy flash,
They zip around with a gnarly dash.
Chasing sun rays like a game of tag,
Their silly moves could make you brag.

"They're coming!" cries from the sandy shore,
Yet all they want is a hug and more.
Splashes fly like they're in a race,
Funny faces, a joyous embrace.

When they gather for lunch, oh what a sight,
Playful bites in the warm sunlight.
Food fights brewing in ocean's trout,
These hunters laugh and swim about!

Teeth of the Midnight Tide

When the moon glows bright and shadows creep,
There's a party lurking in the deep.
Glittering teeth flash with delight,
As they twist and turn in the dead of night.

They grin so wide, it's hard to believe,
Making fish giggle, oh what a weave!
With a twirl and a spin, they steal the show,
Underneath the waves, their charm will grow.

Coffee swirls, and seafoam sways,
These toothy wonders live for plays.
Midnight antics, where laughter roams,
As they shuffle along their watery homes.

So heed the tales of the midnight show,
Where silly bites bring joy to flow.
With happy grins and quite the ride,
In every wave, their fun's worldwide!

Guardians of the Blue

In the azure depths where giggles rise,
Guardians frolic with twinkling eyes.
With chubby cheeks and fins so grand,
They're the jokers in this watery land.

Swapping tales of their best catch,
Of hiding spots and the perfect patch.
With a flip and a flop, they sing along,
Creating the ocean's silliest song.

As they parade with their pearly smiles,
You can't help but laugh for miles.
Guarding the waves, with jest they roam,
Making the ocean a joyful home.

So raise a toast to the playful crew,
Whirling around in the ocean blue.
With laughter echoing in every tide,
They're the guardians of joy, our ocean pride!

Riptide Reveries

In the ocean's grand ballroom, they twirl with flair,
Dressed in sleek suits, with an elegant air.
They nibble on fish, while sharing some laughs,
Practicing their moves, in synchronized halves.

With toothy grins wide, they boast of their speed,
Chasing after bubbles, like a wild stampede.
"Who needs a dance floor?" one hollers with glee,
"We've got the whole ocean, just look at us, see?"

In the heart of the waves, they have a grand feast,
Flipping and flapping, their joy is increased.
They've mastered the art of a silly parade,
While dodging the nets that fishermen made.

As the tide starts to turn, they whirl and they spin,
Making fishy faces, with a toothy grin.
"Let's swim for the shore!" they chant in a cheer,
Riptide revelers, full of joy and good cheer.

The Bite Beneath

Deep in the depths where the waters are dark,
Lives a creature with quite the peculiar spark.
With a toothy grin, it sneaks a sly glance,
And rustles the seaweed, like it's in a dance.

"Oh look, a diver!" it giggles with glee,
"Let's scare him a little, just you wait and see!"
With a flip and a splash, it pops up with flair,
Only to find that the diver don't care!

"Hey there, big fella, is that your best move?
I've seen better tricks from a dolphin's groove!"
The creature just chuckles, a little bit stung,
And swallows its pride, while trying to run.

So next time you dive, and you're met with a grin,
Remember the tales of the creature within.
Not all that you meet want a bite from your leg,
Some just want laughter, like an old-fashioned keg!

An Elegy for the Abyss

In the depths of the ocean, where the sun seldom shines,
Lurks a creature with style, and some funny designs.
With a wiggle and wiggle, it greets passing shells,
And hums to the rhythm of five ocean bells.

"Here lies my snack, a most delicate fish,"
It chuckles aloud, "if only they'd wish!"
But fishes are crafty, they hide in the sand,
This comedic endeavor just slipped from its hand.

With the mermaids all laughing, it takes a deep sigh,
"Why must I always be the butt of the pie?"
But just when it feels like a grand fishy fail,
A crab on the sideline starts to wail and flail!

"Here's to the games we share in the blue,
To the titular roles that we all get to do!
Let's toast to the laughter, to nonsense and fun,
In the heart of the ocean, where troubles weigh none!"

Echoes from the Silent Deeps

In the silence of waters, where the bubbles do play,
Echoes of giggles, a humorous ballet.
Creatures of the deep with their curious flair,
Are scheming and dreaming, while partaking in air.

"Did you hear the one about the fish with two tails?"
The audience chuckles, "Oh, tell us, it pales!"
And as the waves whisper, they gather around,
To share all the laughs that the ocean has found.

Armed with their quips, they swim through the dark,
Joking of corals and barnacles spark.
The playful banter, it sparkles in tune,
Like a raucous party beneath the pale moon.

So next time you ponder the life 'neath the wave,
Remember the laughter, the fun they all crave.
In the depths of the sea, where secrets go deep,
Echoes of joy, in the silence they keep.

Silent Sentinels of the Depths

In tuxedo suits they glide and swirl,
With toothy grins, they dance and twirl.
Beneath the waves, they hold a show,
Critiquing fish with a witty glow.

Their jaws are big, their manners small,
They nibble nibbles—just for fun, after all!
With every flick of their graceful tail,
They send the little ones scurrying pale.

In the ocean's depths, they're on patrol,
Guardians with a playful role.
Haunting the scene, never without flair,
They'll smile at you, if you dare to stare.

So if you see them, don't you fret,
They're just looking for snacks—don't you forget!
Underwater jesters of the bright blue sea,
Bringing laughter to the waves, wild and free.

The Deep's Whispered Roar

Whispers echo through the wave,
While munching lunch, they misbehave.
Jaws pregnant with tales untold,
They giggle silently with teeth of gold.

With a flip and a flop, they glide right by,
Weaving through coral, oh me oh my!
They tell the squids to lighten up,
While chasing minnows in a greasy cup.

A fin pops up like a sail on a ship,
Taking a detour with a playful flip.
Their echoes twist in the salty breeze,
As they find joy in a fishy tease.

In the watery ballroom, they breakdance bold,
Sharing the fun, a sight to behold.
With glimmers of laughter, they take their dive,
Where humor and depth come alive.

Lurkers in the Twilight

At dusk they hover, eyes aglow,
The lapping waves do not know.
With a wink and a jig, they stomp their feet,
Scaring crabs and making them retreat.

Their moods shift with the tides and the flow,
Certain they'd steal the late show.
With every burble, they halo the night,
Casting shadows, scattering delight.

In the twilight's glow, they strut and preen,
A mischief brigade on the ocean's screen.
Playing peek-a-boo with jellyfish sprites,
They spark giggles and childhood delights.

A watchful gaze, a glimmering eye,
Plotting amusing pranks from the sand's sly.
Floating through twilight in a quiet chuckle,
In the arena of bubbles, they shuffle and huddle.

Shadows of the Blue Expanse

In the deep blue, they strut with flair,
A motley crew without a care.
Stealthy and slick, they glide and grin,
Leaving bubbles from where they've been.

With toothy smiles, they lurk all around,
In search of giggles, they plunge downbound.
Holding a party beneath the waves,
Where fish are the guests, and fun raves.

Their shadows dance on the sandy floor,
As they swirl and twirl, asking for more.
Teasing the turtles and tickling the rays,
Jovial jokers in the ocean's bays.

From the sunlit crest to the shadowed hall,
There's always fun at their underwater ball.
Where laughter and bubbles entwine and collide,
Taking a plunge, join the humor tide.

The Abyss Calls

In the depths where the shadows play,
Fins are flapping in a quirky way.
They wear goofy grins, oh what a sight,
Dancing with fish in the pale moonlight.

With bubbles popping, they plot and scheme,
Laughing fishy jokes, living the dream.
Flipping and flopping with silly flair,
Who knew the ocean had such a rare air?

They glide like acrobats, full of glee,
Chasing their tails, living carefree.
Down in the blue, they turn and tease,
Tickling an octopus with such ease.

When the current sways and the tide is right,
They throw a party, it's quite the sight!
Underwater laughter, what a delight,
In the deep blue, hearts feel so light.

Veils of the Salty Abyss

Beneath the waves, a comedy show,
Where the jests and jibes frequently flow.
With a splash and a dash, they tell their tales,
Navigating currents with wobbly gales.

A flounder fakes, as clowns they sway,
With pranks galore, they frolic and play.
Tickling turtles, a feathery jest,
In the salty veil, they're truly blessed.

Their laughter bubbles through gardens of kelp,
Even crabs join in, feeling quite hep.
Seagulls above watch with curious eyes,
As the circus of life takes to the skies.

In this watery realm, they're fantastic fools,
Swimming in circles, breaking the rules.
Splishing and sploshing with all their might,
Veils of the ocean, a hilarious sight!

Seabed Sovereigns

In the kingdom of sand, where the hiders roam,
The rulers wear crowns made of seafoam.
With grinning jaws and playful style,
They reign over coral, each with a smile.

Joking with jellyfish, they dance the night,
Twisting and twirling, what a strange sight!
Turtles applaud with a slow-motion cheer,
As the seabed kings spread laughter near.

Guffaws erupt like bubbles on high,
As the goofy lords wave their fins to the sky.
With a flick of a tail, they tease the future,
Sovereigns of laughter, a joyful suture.

Nowhere to be found is a frown or a sigh,
Just jests and quips as the fish pass by.
In their realm of surface and feathery hue,
Where kings rule in smiles, and fun's always true.

Majesties of the Marianas

In the depths of the fissures, they make their throne,
With noses that wiggle, and scales brightly shone.
Emperors of giggles, they reign with jest,
Making the sea creatures laugh with zest.

In the trench's embrace where the weirdos thrive,
They pull off great stunts, just to survive.
With a splash and a grin, they launch through the gloom,
Creating a ruckus, making flowers bloom.

Beneath the waves, they host epic games,
With squids as contenders and fish with names.
It's a grand spectacle of laughter and cheer,
As the Marianas royals spread joy and good cheer.

As the currents swirl and the waves play their tune,
They dance to the rhythm, beneath the bright moon.
With chuckles and bubbles, they play the right cards,
In their underwater palace, life's sweet rewards.

www.ingramcontent.com/pod-product-compliance
Lightning Source LLC
Chambersburg PA
CBHW060133230426
43661CB00003B/403